Butterflies Are Free

Butterflies
Are Free

by Leonard Gershe

RANDOM HOUSE / NEW YORK

4 6 8 9 7 5 3

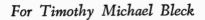

For Timothy Michael Bleck

BUTTERFLIES ARE FREE *was first presented on October 21, 1969, by Arthur Whitelaw, Max J. Brown, Byron Goldman at the Booth Theatre in New York City with the following cast:*

(In order of appearance)

DON BAKER	Keir Dullea
JILL TANNER	Blythe Danner
MRS. BAKER	Eileen Heckart
RALPH AUSTIN	Michael Glaser

Directed by Milton Katselas
Associate Producer Ruth Bailey
Scenery designed by Richard Seger
Lighting by Jules Fisher
Costumes designed by Robert Mackintosh

THE SCENE

*The entire action takes place in Don Baker's apartment
on East 11th Street in New York City.*

ACT ONE

Scene 1: A morning in June.
Scene 2: A few hours later.

ACT TWO

Scene 1: A moment later.
Scene 2: That night.

Act One

SCENE ONE

The scene is DON BAKER's apartment on the top floor of a walk-up on the Lower East Side of Manhattan. There is a skylight, dirty with age. The bed is raised about six and a half feet from the floor, and is reached by a ladder. Under the bed is a door leading to the bathroom. We can

3

make out some posters and photographs pinned to the wall. To the left of the bed is the front door; to the right is the kitchen, with a vintage refrigerator and an old claw-foot bathtub. A slab of wood has been fitted over the tub to serve as a dining table; a couple of stools are around it. Just below the table-tub there is a faded sofa. In front of this is a wood crate which serves as a coffee table, with some cheap chairs around it. There is a telephone on the coffee table. On one wall is a window and a small bookcase. There is a second door, which leads to the next apartment; in front of it is a chest.

Before the curtain rises we hear DON BAKER's *voice singing on a tape recorder: "I knew the day you met me/ I could love you if you let me/ Though you touched my cheek/ And said how easy you'd forget me/ You said* (Improvising) *da-de-da-de-da-da . . ."**

When the curtain rises it is a warm morning in June; the sun is pouring in through the skylight. DON *is leaning against one of the bedposts, drinking a glass of water, and listening to the tape recorder. He is twenty years old, lean and good-looking, wearing a brown button-down shirt and khakis; his hair is combed back and his feet are bare. The phone rings. He moves to the sofa, turns off the tape recorder, looks toward the phone, and speaks to it in a tone indicating he has said this many times.*

4

DON I'm fine, thank you. How are you? (*He goes to the kitchen, and refills his glass with water*) It's warm here. How is it in Scarsdale? (*Goes to the phone*) Well, it's warm here, too. (*Picks up the phone*) Hello, Mother . . . I just knew. When you call, the phone doesn't ring. It just says, "M" is for the million things she gave you . . . I'm fine, thank you. How are you? . . . It's warm here. How is it in Scarsdale? . . . Well, it's warm here, too. The apartment is great. I love it . . . Last night? I didn't do anything last night. I mean I didn't go out. I had some friends in—a little party . . . I don't know how many people were here. Do you have to have a number? Twelve and a half, how's that? . . . No, they didn't stay too late . . . When? No! No, not this afternoon . . . I don't care. Come to town and go to Saks, but you're not coming down here. Because we agreed to two months, didn't we? (*Suddenly the noise of a conversational TV program is heard blaring in the next apartment*) What? . . . No, I didn't turn on my radio. It's coming from next door . . . I don't know . . . a girl . . . She just moved in a couple of days ago . . . I don't know her name. I haven't met her . . . It's her radio . . . Don't worry, it won't go on . . . Yes, I'll tell her . . . No, I don't want you to tell her. Just go to Saks and go home . . . I can hardly hear you. We'll talk tomorrow. Good-bye. (DON *hangs up, goes to the door that connects with the next apartment, and raps angrily*) Hey, would you please . . . (*Knocking louder and shouting*) Would you mind lowering your radio?
(*The TV program is turned off*)

5

JILL (*Offstage*) Sorry. I couldn't hear you.

DON I just wanted you to turn your radio down. You don't have to turn it off. Just lower it, please.

JILL (*Offstage*) I haven't got a radio. It's television.

DON Well, whatever. These walls are made of paper.

JILL (*Offstage*) I know—Kleenex. How about a cup of coffee?

DON No, thanks. I just had some.

JILL (*Offstage*) I meant for me.

DON Sure . . . come on in. (DON *goes to the kitchen and turns on the flame under the coffee pot. There is a knock at the door as he takes a cup and saucer from the cupboard over the sink*) It's open.
    (JILL TANNER *enters. She is nineteen and has a delicate little-girl quality about her. Her long hair falls to her shoulders and down her back. She is wearing an arty blouse and blue jeans. Her blouse zips down the back, and the top of the zipper is open*)

JILL Hi! I'm Jill Tanner.

DON (*Turning toward her and extending his hand*) Don Baker.
    (JILL *shakes his hand*)

JILL I hope you don't mind me inviting myself in. (*Turning her back to him*) Would you do the zipper on my blouse? I can't reach back there. (*There is just*

6

a flash of awkwardness as DON *reaches out for the zipper and zips it up)* Your living room is bigger than mine. How long have you been here?

DON   A month. This isn't the living room. This is the apartment. That's all there is except I have a big bathroom.

JILL   I've got three rooms if you count the kitchen. I just moved in two days ago, but I didn't sign a lease or anything—just by the month. God, you're neat. Everything is so tidy.

DON   It's easy when you haven't got anything.

JILL   *(Looking around)*   I haven't got anything, but it manages to wind up all over the place. I'm afraid I'm a slob. I've heard that boys are neater than girls. *(Looking up)* I like your skylight. I don't have that. *(Moves to the bed)* What's this?

DON   What?

JILL   This thing on stilts.

DON   Oh, my bed.

JILL   *(Climbing the ladder)*   Your bed? Wow! This is WILD!

DON   Do you like it?

JILL   *(Climbing on the bed)*   This is the greatest bed I've ever seen in my life . . . and I've seen a lot of beds. Did you build it?

7

DON No, the guy who lived here before me built it. He was a hippie. He liked to sleep high.

JILL Suppose you fall out? You could break something.

DON You could break something falling out of any bed. (*He pours the coffee into the cup, goes to the coffee table and sets it down*) Cream or sugar?

JILL No, just black.

DON I could have had your apartment, but I took this one because of the bed.

JILL I don't blame you. (*Moving to the sofa*) You know, I buy flowers and dumb things like dishtowels and paper napkins, but I keep forgetting to buy coffee. (JILL *settles on the sofa with her feet beneath her. She picks up the coffee and sips it*)

DON Is it hot enough?

JILL Great. This'll save my life. I'll pay you back some day.

DON You don't have to.

JILL Do you need any dishtowels or paper napkins?

DON No.

JILL I've got lots of light bulbs, too—everything but coffee. May I ask you a personal question?

DON Sure.

8

JILL   Why don't you want your mother to come here?

DON   How did you know that?

JILL   If you can hear me, I can hear you. I think the sound must go right under that door. What's that door for, anyway?

DON   Your apartment and mine were once one apartment. When they converted it into two, they just locked that door instead of sealing it up. I guess in case they want to make it one again.

JILL   You didn't answer my question.

DON   I forgot what you asked.

JILL   Why don't you want your mother here?

DON   It's a long story. No, it's a short story—it's just been going on a long time. She didn't want me to leave home. She thinks I can't make it on my own. Finally, we agreed to letting me try it for two months. She's to keep away from me for two months. I've got a month to go.

JILL   Why did you tell her you had a party last night?

DON   Boy, you don't miss anything in there, do you?

JILL   Not much.

DON   I always tell her I've had a party . . . or went to one. She wouldn't understand why I'd rather be here alone than keeping her and the cook company. She'll hate this place. She hates it now without even seeing it.

9

She'll walk in and the first thing she'll say is, "I could absolutely cry!"

JILL   Does she cry a lot?

DON   No—she just threatens to.

JILL   If she really wants to cry, send her in to look at my place. At least you're neat. You're old enough to live alone, aren't you? I'm nineteen. How old are you?

DON   As far as my mother's concerned, I'm still eleven— going on ten.

JILL   We must have the same mother. Mine would love me to stay a child all my life—or at least all *her* life. So *she* won't age. She loves it when people say we look like sisters. If they don't say it, she tells them. Have you got a job?

DON   Not yet . . . but I play the guitar, and I've got a few prospects.

JILL   I heard you last night.

DON   Sorry.

JILL   No, it was good. First I thought it was a record till you kept playing one song over and over.

DON   I can't read music, so I have to learn by ear. I'm trying to put together an act.

JILL   Then what?

DON Then I'll try to cash in on some of those prospects. I know one thing—I ain't a-goin' back to Scarsdale.

JILL What is Scarsdale?

DON You don't know Scarsdale?

JILL I don't know much about the East. I'm from Los Angeles.

DON Scarsdale's just outside of New York—about twenty miles.

JILL Is that where you live?

DON No, I live here. It's where I used to live.

JILL Scars-dale. It sounds like a sanitarium where they do plastic surgery. Is there any more coffee?

DON (*Putting his cigarette out in the ashtray*) Plenty.

JILL I can get it.

DON (*Rises and holds out his hand for the cup*) I'm up. (JILL *hands him the cup. He goes to the kitchen to pour her more coffee*) What did you say your name is?

JILL Jill Tanner. Technically, I guess I'm Mrs. Benson. I was married once . . . when I was sixteen.

DON Sixteen! Did you have your parents' permission?

JILL My mother's. I told her I was pregnant, but I wasn't. She cried her eyes out. She hated the thought of becoming a grandmother. I'll bet I know what you're thinking.

DON What?

(DON *returns, sets the cup on the table, and resumes his seat*)

JILL You're thinking I don't look like a *divorcée*.

DON No, I wasn't thinking that. What does a divorcée look like?

JILL Oh, you know. They're usually around thirty-five with tight-fitting dresses and high-heel patent leather shoes and big boobs. I look more like the kid in a custody fight.

DON How long were you married?

JILL God, it seemed like weeks! Actually, it was six days. (*She lights a cigarette*) It wasn't Jack's fault. It wasn't anybody's fault. It was just one of those terrible mistakes you make before you can stop yourself, even though you know it's a mistake while you're doing it.

DON What was he like?

JILL Jack? Oh . . . (*Uncomfortably*) I really can't talk about him.

DON Then don't. I'm sorry.

JILL No, I will talk about him. Once in a while it's good for you to do something you don't want to do. It cleanses the insides. He was terribly sweet and groovy-looking, but kind of adolescent, you know what I mean? Girls mature faster than boys. Boys are neater, but girls mature faster. When we met it was like fireworks and rockets. I don't know if I'm saying it right, but it was a marvelous kind of passion that made every day like the Fourth of July. Anyway, the next thing I knew we were standing in front of a justice of the peace getting married.

DON   How long had you known him?

JILL   Two or three weeks, but I mean there we were getting *married!* I hadn't even finished high school and I had two exams the next day and they were on my mind, too. I heard the justice of the peace saying, "Do you, *Jack*, take Jill to be your lawfully wedded wife?" Can you imagine going through life as Jack and Jill? And then I heard "Till death do you part," and suddenly it wasn't a wedding ceremony. It was a funeral service.

DON   (*Lighting a cigarette*)   Jesus!

JILL   You know, that wedding ceremony is very morbid when you think about it. I hate anything morbid and there I was being buried alive . . . under Jack Benson. I wanted to run screaming out into the night!

DON   Did you?

JILL   I couldn't. It was ten o'clock in the morning. I mean you can't go screaming out into ten o'clock in the morning—so I passed out. If only I'd fainted before I said "I do."

DON As long as you were married, why didn't you try to make it work?

JILL I did try—believe me. (*She picks up an ashtray and holds it in her hand*) I tried for six days, but I knew it was no good.

DON Were you in love with him?
(DON *flicks an ash from his cigarette onto the table where the ashtray had been before* JILL *moved it.* JILL *reacts to this fleetingly, and shrugs it off*)

JILL In my way.

DON What's your way?

JILL I don't know . . . Well, I think just because you love someone, that doesn't necessarily mean that you want to spend the rest of your life with him. But Jack loved me. I mean he really, really loved me, and I hurt him and that's what I can't stand. I just never want to hurt anybody. I mean marriage is a commitment, isn't it? I just can't be committed or involved. Can you understand?

DON I understand, but I don't agree.
(DON *flicks his ashes onto the table*)

JILL Then you don't understand really. (JILL *looks at him, oddly*) What is this? Maybe I've got it wrong. Maybe boys mature faster and girls are neater.

DON What do you mean?

JILL Or maybe you know something I don't know—like

ashes are good for the table? Is that why you keep dropping them there?

DON   Did you move the ashtray?

JILL   (*Holding up the ashtray beside her*)   It's right here. Are you blind?

DON   Yes.

JILL   What do you mean *yes*?

DON   I mean yes. I'm blind.

JILL   You're putting me on.

DON   No, I'm blind. I've always been blind.

JILL   Really blind? Not just near-sighted?

DON   The works. I can't see a thing.
(JILL *leans over and runs her hands across* DON's *eyes. When he doesn't blink, she realizes he is indeed blind*)

JILL   God! I hope I didn't say anything . . .

DON   Now, don't get self-conscious about it. I'm not.

JILL   Why didn't you tell me?

DON   I just did.

JILL   I mean when I came in.

DON   You didn't ask me.

JILL   Why would I ask? I mean I don't go into someone's house and say, "Hi, I'm Jill Tanner—are you
blind?"

DON   Right. And I don't meet a stranger and say, "Hi,
Don Baker—blind as a bat."

JILL   I think you should've told me. I would've told
you.

DON   Well . . . I wanted to see how long it would take
for you to catch on. Now you know. Do you want to
run screaming out into the night or just faint?

JILL   How can you make jokes?

DON   Listen, the one thing that drives me up the wall is
pity. I don't want it and I don't need it. Please—don't
feel sorry for me. I don't feel sorry for me, so why
should you?

JILL   You're so . . . adjusted.

DON   No, I'm not. I never *had* to adjust. I was born blind.
It might be different if I'd been able to see and then
went blind. For me, blindness is normal. I was six years
old before I found out everyone else wasn't blind. By
that time it didn't make much difference. So, let's relax
about it. Okay? And if we can have a few laughs, so
much the better.

JILL   A few laughs? About *blindness*?

DON   No, not about blindness. Can't you just forget that?

JILL   I don't know. You're the first blind person I've ever met.

DON   Congratulations. Too bad they don't give out prizes for that.

JILL   I've seen blind men on the street—you know, with dogs. Why don't you have a dog?

DON   They attract too much attention. I'd rather do it myself.

JILL   But isn't it rough getting around New York? It is for me!

DON   Not at all. I manage very well with my cane. I've got so I know exactly how many steps to take to the grocery . . . the laundry . . . the drugstore.

JILL   Where's a laundry? I need one.

DON   Next to the delicatessen. Forty-four steps from the front door.

JILL   I didn't see it.

DON   I'll show it to you.

JILL   What about here in the apartment? Aren't you afraid of bumping into everything? You could hurt yourself.

DON   I've memorized the room. (*Moves around the room with grace and confidence, calling off each item as he*

touches it or points to it) Bed . . . bathroom . . .
bookcase . . . guitar . . . my cane.
   *(He holds up the white aluminum walking stick,
   then puts it back on the shelf)*

JILL   What are those books?

DON   Braille . . . Front door . . . tape recorder. *(Moving
on)* Dining table . . . bathtub. *(Walks quickly to the
chest of drawers against the door to* JILL's *apartment)*
Chest of drawers. *(Touching the things on top)* Wine
. . . more wine . . . glasses. *(He opens the top drawer)*
Linens. *(Closes the drawer; opens the front door and
shuts it; moves on to the kitchen)* Kitchen . . . *(He
opens the cabinet over the sink)* Dishes . . . cups . . .
glasses. *(He opens the next cabinet)* Coffee . . .
sugar . . . salt and pepper . . . corn flakes . . . ketchup
. . . etcetera. *(Returning to* JILL*)* Now, if you'll put
the ashtray back. *(She replaces the ashtray on the
table, and* DON *stamps out his cigarette in it. He sits on
the sofa and holds out his arms with bravura)* Voilà!
If you don't move anything, I'm as good as anyone
else.

JILL   Better. God, I can't find anything in my place. The
ketchup usually winds up in my stocking drawer and
my stockings are in the oven. If you really want to see
chaos, come and look at . . . *(She catches herself,
self-consciously)* I mean . . . I meant . . .

DON   I know what you mean. Relax. I'm no different
from anyone else except that I don't see. The blindness
is nothing. The thing I find hard to live with is other
people's reactions to my blindness. If they'd only
behave naturally. Some people want to assume guilt—
which they can't because my mother has that market

cornered—or they treat me as though I were living in some Greek tragedy, which I assure you I'm not. Just be yourself.

JILL I'll try . . . but I've never met a blind person before.

DON That's because we're a small, very select group—like Eskimos. How many Eskimos do you know?

JILL I never thought blind people would be like you.

DON They're not all like me. We're all different.

JILL I mean . . . I always thought blind people were kind of . . . you know . . . spooky.

DON (In a mock-sinister voice) But, of course. We sleep all day hanging upside-down from the shower rod. As soon as it's dark, we wake up and fly into people's windows. That's why they say, "Blind as a bat."

JILL No, seriously . . . don't blind people have a sixth sense?

DON No. If I had six senses, I'd still have only five, wouldn't I? My other senses—hearing, touch, smell— maybe they're a little more developed than yours, but that's only because I use them more. I have to.

JILL Boy, I think it's just so great that you aren't bitter. You don't seem to have any bitterness at all. (She shifts to sitting on the sofa, burying her feet under a cushion) I've moved. I'm sitting on the sofa now.

DON I know.

JILL   How did you know?

DON   I heard you—and your voice is coming from a different spot.

JILL   Wow! How do you do it?

DON   It's easy. Close your eyes and listen. (*He tiptoes to another part of the room*) You know where I am?

JILL   There. Hey, it works. You're really something. I think I'd be terribly bitter if I couldn't see. I'd sure be disagreeable.

DON   No, you wouldn't.

JILL   I couldn't be cheerful like you. I don't have any marvelous qualities like courage and fortitude.

DON   Neither have I. I'm just naturally adorable.

JILL   You're more than that. I can tell you're a much better person than I am.

DON   Are you speaking to me or Gunga Din?

JILL   I would not "go gentle into that good night." I would "rage against the dying of the light."

DON   Dylan Thomas.

JILL   Who?

DON   That's a line from a poem by Dylan Thomas.

JILL (*Delightfully surprised*) It is? You mean I can quote from Dylan Thomas?

DON You just did.

JILL How about that! I've never even read him. I don't know where I learned it. I can quote Mark Twain. Do you want to hear my favorite quotation? It's by Mark Twain.

DON Go ahead.

JILL (*Reciting*) "I only ask to be free. The butterflies are free. Mankind will surely not deny to Harold Skimpole what it concedes to the butterflies." (*Resuming her normal tone*) I identify, strongly, with butterflies. Do you like that quotation?

DON Yes, but it's not by Mark Twain.

JILL Why not?

DON Because it was written by Charles Dickens.

JILL Are you sure?

DON Yes. Harold Skimpole is a character in *Bleak House* by Dickens.

JILL I've never read Dickens. Actually, I've never read anything by Mark Twain, either, but I always thought he wrote that. Have you read . . . (*Gasping*) Oh, God!

DON (*He crosses the room to get his guitar*) Yes, I've

read Dickens and most of the things by Mark Twain, and stop falling apart with every word. They're published in braille.

JILL   But it's awful to ask someone blind if he's read something.

DON   As a matter of fact, I read very well—with my fingertips. Just ask me if I've felt any good books lately.

JILL   Do people ever read to you?

DON   Yes—magazines and newspapers.

JILL   Would you like me to read to you sometime?

DON   Sure—but don't feel you have to. Say, do you have any dirty books?

JILL   No.

DON   Too bad—that's the only thing they don't publish in braille.

JILL   Which magazines do you like?

DON   Things like *Time* and *Newsweek*. I like to know what's going on in the world.

JILL   I should read those, too. I never know what's going on in the world. I guess I don't care.

DON   Don't say that. Animals care. Vegetables don't. You have to care about something or you're nothing.

JILL   Food.

DON   You care about food?

JILL   I think about it a lot.

DON   I suppose that's something.

JILL   You have to know a lot about things to care about them, and I don't really know a lot about anything.

DON   You sure don't need any enemies, do you?

JILL   Let's say I know my limitations.

DON   That's half the battle. If you know your limitations, you can do something about them. I think you have a lot more potential than you know.

JILL   Keep telling me that.

DON   Keep telling yourself that. (*He strums his guitar and sings*)
    I knew the day you met me
    I could love you if you let me,
    Though you touched my cheek
    And said how easy you'd forget me,
    You said, "Butterflies are free
    And so are we."

JILL   Oh, wow. That's wonderful. That's the song you were singing last night.

DON I wrote it. I've been working on it, but I could never get those last lines right. What do you think?

JILL It's terrific! I know a little about music. I studied in school.

DON Did you finish school?

JILL I finished high school—*just*. My mother wanted me to go to college. I was going to U.C.L.A., but I couldn't find a place to park. Have you ever been to L.A.?

DON No. I hear the climate is great.

JILL The climate is great, but the weather is lousy. I guess it's a good place to live—with gardens and pools and all that. I like it better here. People say New York is a great place to visit, but they wouldn't want to live here. What could be groovier than living in a place that's great to visit?

DON What made you come here?

JILL Nothing *made* me come. I just thought I'd like to try something different. I think I'm going to be an actress. I say I think. I'll know later this afternoon. I'm reading for a part in a new off-Broadway play.

DON Good part?

JILL I guess so. It's the lead. It's about a girl who gets all hung up because she's married a homosexual. Originally he was an alcoholic, but homosexuals are very "in" now, so they changed it. Are you homosexual?

DON No—just blind.

JILL They are in everything now—books, plays, movies.
It's really too bad. I always thought of them as kind of
magical and mysterious—the greatest secret society in
the world. Now they're telling all the secrets and you
find out they're just like everybody else—mixed up and
sad. Do you know any homosexuals?

DON I doubt it. I've been in Scarsdale all my life.

JILL One of my best friends is gay. Dennis. He's a
designer. He made this blouse.
(She holds her blouse out for DON *to see, then
winces to herself)*

DON I'm sure it's pretty.

JILL Actually, he made it for himself, but I talked him
out of it. Dennis is campy and fun, but I don't like
lesbians. They're so heavy and humorless. If guys are
called "gay," the girls should be called "glum."

DON Tell me about the play. Does the girl convert the
husband?

JILL Almost, but in the end he runs off with her
brother.

DON So her husband becomes her sister-in-law.

JILL Something like that. Or she becomes her own sister-in-law. I have a good chance of getting the part.
The director is a friend of mine, but I have to be ap-
proved by the author.

DON Who's the director?

JILL You wouldn't know him. His name is Ralph Austin. He's done a few plays here, but never had a hit. He started in L.A. doing off-Broadway shows on Hollywood Boulevard.

DON That's what I call off-Broadway.

JILL We kind of made it together for a few months, but then he wanted to get married. I just couldn't face that again.

DON Were you in love with him?

JILL I don't think I've ever really been in love with anyone. I don't want to be. It's so . . . confining and somebody always gets hurt. Are you hungry?

DON Not very. Are you?

JILL Always. My appetite embarrasses me. I told you I think about food a lot . . . and care deeply. Why don't I go down to the delicatessen and get something? I know exactly where it is—forty-four steps from the front door.

DON That's the laundry. The delicatessen is fifty-one steps. *(He rises)* I've got things to eat.

JILL What have you got?

DON Some bologna and salami and potato salad—and I think there's some coleslaw.

JILL Boy, you *are* a delicatessen. Can you shop for yourself?

DON Sure.

JILL I mean, I know you can tell a dime from a quarter, but how do you know the difference between a dollar bill and a five?
(DON *takes his wallet from his hip pocket and takes out a bill*)

DON This is a single. Right?

JILL How do you know?

DON Because it's folded once. If it were a five, I'd fold it again . . . like this. (*He folds the bill again*) And a ten I'd fold once more. (*He folds the bill again to demonstrate, then unfolds it and puts it back in his wallet*) Got it?

JILL What about twenties?

DON Who's got twenties?
(DON *crosses to the kitchen and sets about putting the food on plates*)

JILL Can I do something?

DON There are some knives and forks in the chest of drawers. You can set the table.

JILL (*Crossing to the chest*) Let's don't eat at the table. Let's have a picnic.

DON Where?

JILL   On the floor.

DON   Okay, set the floor.
(JILL *takes the silverware and a small cloth from the chest, and sets them out on the floor in front of the coffee table*)

JILL   Is blindness hereditary?

DON   I've never heard that.

JILL   Can your father see?

DON   I doubt it. He's been dead for six years. Up till then he didn't have any trouble.

JILL   I'll bet you miss him.

DON   (*Nodding sadly*) Very much. He was the only friend I had growing up. He was the kind of man who would have been my friend even if he hadn't been my father. You know what I mean. But it's been rough on Mom since he died because Mom felt she had to be mother *and* father . . . and sister and brother and cousin and uncle and doctor and lawyer . . . Senator . . . Congressman . . .

JILL   I've got it. Why were you born blind? Did the doctor say why?

DON   They said it was a virus in the womb when mother was pregnant—which means they don't know. Whenever they don't know something, they label it "virus."

JILL   I've heard that women with syphilis will give birth to blind babies. Could your mother have had syphilis?

DON Wait till you meet her, then tell me what *you* think.

JILL When will I meet her?

DON In a month. I've got one month before she comes down here to see what's going on. As the clock strikes month, she'll walk in the door. You may have heard of her. She wrote some books. Her name is Florence Baker.

JILL It's not familiar—but you can't go by me. I could be quoting her and wouldn't know it.

DON They were a series of children's books. Guess what they were about?

JILL Children?

DON A blind kid named Little Donny Dark.

JILL (*Incredulously*) Little Donny Dark?

DON That's me.

JILL Boy, you'll say anything to get attention!

DON It's true, I swear. I hate that name—Donny. (*He carries the plates toward the center of the room*) Tell me when to stop.

JILL Stop. (DON *stops at the edge of the cloth, kneels, and sets the plates down. He sits with his legs crossed under him.* JILL *gets up*) Just a minute.

DON Where are you going?

JILL   You'll see. (*She rushes out the front door, and returns a moment later with a small basket of flowers which she offers to* DON *to smell. He smiles.* JILL *places the flowers in the center of the picnic, stretches out on her stomach and digs into the food*) Tell me about Little Donny Dark. It might curb my appetite.

DON   Donny is twelve years old and was born blind like me, only it's no handicap to Little Donny Dark. He can drive cars and fly planes, 'cause, you see, his other faculties are so highly developed that he can hear a bank being robbed a mile away and he can smell the Communists cooking up a plot to overthrow the government. He's a diligent fighter of crime and injustice, and at the end of every book, as he is being given a medal from the police or the C.I.A. or the F.B.I., he always says, "There are none so blind as those who will not see!"

JILL   I didn't know the police and the F.B.I. gave out medals.

DON   They give 'em to Little Donny Dark. They'd better!

JILL   Boy! Let's have a drink.

DON   (*Rising*)   I've only got wine.

JILL   That's all I drink.

DON   With bologna?

JILL   With everything.
(DON *crosses to the chest, passing behind the sofa*)

30

JILL Do children really read those books?

DON (*Stopping*) Shh! I'm counting—so I don't step in the picnic when I come back. (DON *continues to the chest, takes a bottle of wine which has been opened, and some glasses.* JILL *watches, in awe, as he returns and stops, precisely at the edge of the cloth*) Nine steps.
(*He sits, placing the bottle and glasses on the cloth.* JILL *pours the wine*)

JILL I could never do that. I'd wind up with both feet in the coleslaw.

DON No, you wouldn't.

JILL I speak from experience. Did you ever play Pin the Tail on the Donkey?

DON I've heard of it.

JILL We always played it at birthday parties when I was a kid. I remember Julie Patterson's birthday. I guess I was about seven. I was blindfolded and started for the donkey, and stuck the pin smack into Mrs. Patterson's ass.

DON Well, donkey . . . ass, it's all the same, isn't it?

JILL Not to Mrs. Patterson it wasn't. She never believed I didn't do it on purpose. I didn't. I didn't have to. I mean if you knew Mrs. Patterson's ass—well, you couldn't miss it—just no way. But *you'd've* won every prize there. My language gets a little raunchy sometimes. I hope you don't mind four-letter words like

31

"ass." (*She takes a long swig of wine*) I'm ready for more.

DON   More what?

JILL   Little Donny Dark. Is she still writing them?

DON   No. She wrote about six. They were pretty popular—no Mary Poppins, but pretty popular . . . (*Wryly*) Unless you happened to be blind. They didn't exactly tell it like it is.

JILL   (*Takes a slice of meat from* DON's *plate, having finished her own*) I'm taking some of your bologna.

DON   I guess the books were sort of a projection of what my mother hoped I'd be—a sightless superman.

JILL   Where did you go to school?

DON   In the living room. I was taught by tutors who teach the blind.

JILL   I thought there were schools for blind children.

DON   There are, but I didn't know that. I didn't know much of anything until about a year ago.

JILL   (*Spears a piece of* DON's *bologna with her fork*) You've just finished your bologna. What happened a year ago?

DON   (*Rising*) A family named Fletcher moved near us and their daughter, Linda, used to come by to read to me. She was the first friend I had after my father died. She was great—a swinger. She used to drive me down here and introduce me to people and take me to parties. All of a sudden, I was living—and learning. At home I was like a pet in a cage. Linda gave me something nobody ever thought to give me—confidence. She talked me into making the break and she found this place for me. At first I was scared to death, but I did it. Maybe it was a mistake . . . I don't know.

JILL (*Rising*) No, it wasn't. You've got to do it sometime. Your mother isn't going to live forever.

DON Don't tell her that.

JILL God, look at someone like Helen Keller. She was blind and deaf and dumb, but she became . . . Helen Keller. What became of Linda?

DON She got married a few weeks ago and she's living in Chicago. I wish she were here. It would be a lot easier.

JILL Well, listen, I'm here. I'm right next door. Any time you need me, just knock. You don't even have to knock. Just whisper and I can hear you. (*She looks over at her door*) Hey—you know what?

DON What?

JILL (*Jumping up*) Why don't we open that door?

DON Which door?

JILL That door to my apartment. There must be a key for it. Let's unlock it. Then we can go back and forth without going out in the hall.

DON The super probably has a key, but I don't think we ought to ask him. No, I don't think we ought to do that.

JILL Why not? We're friends, aren't we?

DON But we'd be practically living together. How would it look? (*Excitedly, answering his own question*) Who cares how it looks? I can't see, anyway!

JILL (*She goes to the kitchen, finds a sharp knife, and returns to her door*) I'll bet we can open it with this big knife.

DON We'll have to move the chest.
(*They grab the edges of the chest*)

JILL Move it toward you. (*They move the chest away from the door*) That's fine.
(*JILL sets her end of the chest down and rushes at the lock with the knife. She maneuvers it around, but nothing happens*)

DON What's on the other side?

JILL My bedroom. This isn't working. Boy, a burglar can just smile at a lock and it opens, but honest people like you and me . . . Tsk!

DON I heard something click.

JILL That was me. I went "tsk!" Damn! Maybe we'd better call the super.

DON Let me try. (*JILL places the knife in DON's hand. He feels for the lock and maneuvers the knife around in it, then takes the knife from the lock and delicately works it between the door and the lock)* I felt something.

(JILL *tries the door. It opens)*

JILL You did it! It's open! (*We can see part of* JILL's *bedroom with a lot of her things strewn about untidily. She closes the door quickly, embarrassed)* Oh, don't look! It's an absolute pigsty!

DON (*Covering his eyes and turning away)* I won't.

JILL (*Sinking)* I'm sorry.

DON Stop being sorry.

JILL I'll get the hang of it. I just don't know when. (DON *tries the door to see which way it opens. It opens into* JILL's *apartment)*

JILL Let's leave it open.

DON (*Going to the kitchen to put the knife away)* Tell me if you close the door so I won't break my nose on it. (JILL *perches on the back of the sofa)*

JILL Do you wish it were Linda living there instead of me?

DON I never even thought about it. Why do you ask?

JILL I was wondering if you're still in love with her.

DON Did I say I was in love with her?

35

JILL   If I get too personal, just tell me to shut up. I get carried away. Were you in love with her? Are you?

DON   Every man should have some mystery about him. That'll be mine.

JILL   What's she like?

DON   She's very pretty.

JILL   How do you know?

DON   I can feel someone's face and get a good idea of what they look like. I can tell from shapes and textures.

JILL   Do you wonder what I look like?

DON   Yes.

JILL   I'm gorgeous.

DON   Really?

JILL   I wouldn't lie about something like that.

DON   You know, I've always thought if I could see for just half a minute I'd like to see how I look.

JILL   I'll tell you. Cute . . . and very sexy.
      (DON smiles and reaches a hand toward JILL's face. She takes his hand and places it on her cheek. Gently, he runs his finger up the side of her face, exploring. He runs his hand over the top of her head and takes hold of her long hair, lightly pulling it through his fingers)

36

DON Your hair is very soft . . . and very long. (*Suddenly,* JILL's *long hair—which is really a fall—comes off in* DON's *hand, revealing her own short hair underneath.* DON *is startled as he feels the limp hair in his hand*) Oh, Jesus!
(*He falls back on the sofa*)

JILL Don't be frightened.

DON (*Dropping the fall like a hot potato*) What happened?
(JILL *picks up the fall and sits beside him*)

JILL It's a fall. It's a piece of long hair that you attach to your head.

DON It's not *your* hair?

JILL It's not even my fall. I borrowed it from Susan Potter. I do have hair of my own. See? I mean, feel? (*She places his hand on her head.* DON *takes in the shape of her head, then moves his hand along her face, over her eyes. A false eyelash comes off in his hand*)

DON God! Now what?

JILL (*Takes the eyelash from him and puts it back on*) That's just a false eyelash.

DON Don't you have eyelashes?

JILL Of course, but these make your eyes look bigger. They're longer than mine. Didn't Linda wear them?

DON No.

37

JILL   She probably has naturally long lashes. I hate her. (*Placing his hand on her cheek*) Go on.

DON   This is scaring hell out of me.

JILL   It's all right. Everything's real from now on. (DON *runs his fingers across* JILL's *mouth*) Am I not the image of Elizabeth Taylor?

DON   I've never felt Elizabeth Taylor.

JILL   We look exactly alike. Especially if you can't see. (JILL *smiles at* DON, *oddly, as his fingers explore her throat. She takes his hand and places it on her breast*) That's my breast. All mine. Both of them. (*Gently, she pushes him down on the sofa and gets on top of him. She kisses him full on the mouth, then raises herself and starts to unbutton his shirt. She continues un-buttoning as she leans down to kiss him again.* DON *twists his head away from her, suddenly, anguished*) What's the matter?

DON   What do you think is the matter?

JILL   If I knew I wouldn't ask.

DON   Why are you doing this? Is it "Be Kind to the Handicapped Week" or something? (*Raising himself on one elbow*) Don't patronize me! And don't feel sorry for me!

JILL   (*Hotly*) I'm doing it because I want to do it! And I'll be goddamned if I feel sorry for any guy who's going to have sex with me!
   (DON's *hand is on her shoulder now. The lights fade, slowly. The curtain is lowered to denote the*

passing of a few hours. We can hear DON *playing the guitar and singing: "On that velvet morning/ When our love was forming/ I said it wouldn't hurt me/ if you left without warning/ I said, 'Butterflies are free/ And so are we'")*

When the curtain rises the remnants of the picnic lunch are still on the floor. JILL'*s blouse and jeans lie in a heap nearby. Her fall is on the coffee table.* DON'*s shirt and trousers are hanging over the back of a chair.* DON, *dressed only in his jockey shorts, is on the sofa, playing his guitar and singing.* JILL *calls from her apartment.*

JILL (*Offstage*)   I can't find it. I can't find anything in this mess.

DON   What are you looking for?

JILL (*Offstage*)   Never mind. It's here somewhere.
(DON *continues to play.* JILL *enters from her apartment, dressed only in panties and bra, and carrying a box a little larger than a cigar box, made of beautiful wood and mother-of-pearl. She curls up on the sofa beside* DON)

JILL   I found it.

DON   What is it?

JILL   My secret box. I take it with me everywhere. Here. Feel it.
(JILL *places* DON'*s hand on the box. He runs his fingers over it*)

DON   Beautiful wood.

JILL   And mother-of-pearl.

DON *(Smiling)*   What do you keep in it?

JILL   *(Opening the box and rummaging through it)*
Everything important to me. *(She takes out a small
piece of rock)* This is a piece of the moon or a star.
(She places it in DON's *hand)* I found it in the desert.
I showed it to a geologist who said he'd never seen
any mineral like it on earth, and it probably fell here
from the moon or maybe a star.

DON   It feels like a rock.

JILL   *(Taking it and putting it back in the box)*   I know,
but it isn't. *(She takes out a baby tooth and holds it
up)* One of my baby teeth. *(She puts the tooth back
and rummages through some papers)* My birth certif-
icate . . . A picture of me when I was in *The Mikado*
in high school. It's not very good anyway . . . my last
will and testament.

DON   Your last will and testament?

JILL   *(Holding up a sheet of yellow foolscap paper)*
And the instructions for my funeral. My entire estate
is to be divided, equally, among whoever are my four
closest friends when I die. Names to be filled in later.

DON   I thought you didn't like anything morbid.

JILL   But that's the point. It isn't morbid. Funerals
don't have to be morbid. I want mine in a large church,
but I want all the pews and seats removed and just lots
of big cushions for people to lie on. I don't want anyone dressed in black. They should all be in gay, bright
colors and far-out clothes and they should all be drink-

ing or smoking pot or whatever they like. I want Salvador Dali to paint the walls with lots of groovy pictures and I want tons of flowers, but not formal wreaths. Just tons of wild flowers strewn everywhere.

DON Butterflies?

JILL Oh, yes, lots of butterflies. And I want music going all the time. I want the Beatles to write a special memoriam for me and to sing it. And I want the Rolling Stones to sing and Simon and Garfunkle and the Doors and the Vienna Boys' Choir.

DON And me . . .

JILL . . . and you . . .

DON How about a eulogy?

JILL Yes—to be delivered by Sidney Poitier. I love his voice. And at the same time I want André Previn playing "Ave Maria" on the organ. If he can't come, maybe Leonard Bernstein. There's nothing morbid about that, is there?

DON Not at all.

JILL (*Taking some hippie beads from the box*) Oh, here it is! A present for you.
(*She slips the beads over his neck*)

DON What is it?

JILL What does it feel like?

DON A necklace.

42

JILL   They're love beads. I wore them when I was a hippie. You ought to wear beads if you're going to play the guitar.

DON   Nobody told me.

JILL   Donovan wears them . . . and Jimi Hendrix.

DON   What else should I wear?

JILL   (*Rising as she studies him*)   Oh, some kicky clothes —wild. And your hair doesn't exactly blow the mind.

DON   What's wrong with it?

JILL   I can fix it.
        (*She runs into her apartment*)

DON   What's wrong with it?

JILL   (*Offstage*)   The way you comb it.
        (JILL *returns, carrying her purse, and looking through it*)

JILL   It's a little square. I can fix it. I know I have a comb here. (*She looks toward the kitchen*) Is there anything left to eat? I'm starving.

DON   So soon?

JILL   Isn't it awful?

DON   There should be a couple of apples.
        (JILL *tucks the purse under her arm and rushes to the refrigerator. She opens it and peers in*)

43

JILL There's an awful lot of lettuce—which is not exactly what I was dreaming of. I only see one apple.
(She takes the apple out)

DON It's yours.

JILL Thanks. *(She returns to the sofa with the apple in her mouth, and searches through her purse. She produces a comb and a small pair of scissors. When she runs the comb through DON's hair, he is startled)* Just sit still. I'm very good at this.

DON I don't know that I want to look like a hippie.

JILL You're not going to look like a hippie. You're going to look hip.
(She settles on the sofa arm and proceeds to do his hair over, combing it forward and snipping at it as she eats her apple)

DON When were you a hippie?

JILL I guess it was right after my marriage. I used to hang around the Sunset Strip and smoke pot and say things like "Down with the fuzz" and "Don't trust anyone over thirty." The whole bit. I just did it because everybody was doing it. Then I stopped because everybody was doing it. I felt I was losing my individuality—whatever that is. The main thing, of course, was to protest against my mother, but it didn't work. I mean I walked in one day with my hair long and stringy, wearing far-out clothes and beads and sandals . . . and she LOVED it! Next day, *she* had stringy hair and far-out clothes and beads and sandals. Well, I mean how can you protest against someone who's

44

doing the same thing you are? Right? So, I went the other way and joined the Young Republicans for Ronald Reagan. Another mistake. There's no such thing as a young Republican. (*She finishes with his hair and studies it*) There. You look terrific.

(*Without thinking, she takes a small mirror from her bag and holds it up in front of his face. Realizing her mistake, she makes a face to herself and slips the mirror back into her bag*)

DON It doesn't look too wild, does it?

JILL I think it looks great. It gives you charisma.

DON What do you mean—charisma?

JILL It's like pizazz. Star quality. It's better than talent. If you have charisma you don't need anything else. They'll line up for blocks to see you. (*She looks at him for a moment, then kisses him, gently, on the lips*) You're beautiful, you know? I mean you're a beautiful person inside as well as out.

DON (*Smiling*) I like you, too.

JILL I feel I ought to tell you something.

DON What?

JILL Well, before . . . when I took your hand and put it on my breast . . . were you shocked?

DON Sort of. I don't mean from the standpoint of morals or anything. I was just surprised to be feeling a girl's breast when I wasn't expecting to.

JILL   I wouldn't like you to think that I go around putting men's hands on my breast.

DON   No, I don't think you go around doing that.

JILL   If I want to go to bed with a guy . . . usually I have a little smile that lets him know I'm interested.

DON   (*Reaching his hand out*)   Smile that smile. I want to feel it.

JILL   (*Tries her come-hither smile, but starts to giggle helplessly*)   I can't. You're making me laugh.

DON   (*Running his fingers across her laughing mouth*)   Is that it?

JILL   No, of course not. Oh, I can't do it now. I'll do it later. But I had to use a different approach with you, didn't I? Well, I didn't want you to think I was terrible.

DON   I didn't. I don't.

JILL   I hate talking about sex, but I thought maybe you'd like to know that you're . . . well, really groovy.

DON   (*Smiling*)   Like the Fourth of July?

JILL   Like the Fourth of July—and like Christmas.

DON   Where are you going?

JILL   I'm going to throw the apple core away—and maybe I'll have some lettuce.
      As JILL *crosses to the kitchen to throw away the*

apple core, DON *rises and starts up the ladder to his bed. The door opens quietly and* MRS. BAKER *enters. She is an attractive, well-dressed woman, carrying a Saks Fifth Avenue box. She smiles at* DON *silently.* JILL, *in an effort to hide her near-nudity, bumps into a waste basket noisily.* MRS. BAKER *turns to look at her for a moment; she completes the turn, looking back at* DON *with disapproval.* DON *sits on his bed, aware of someone new in the room)*

DON *(Sagging)* Hello, Mother!
(Blackout)

Curtain

Act Two

SCENE ONE

The scene is the same, a moment later. DON *is sitting on the sofa, gritting his teeth and trying not to show his annoyance.* JILL *is still peeking out from behind the shutters.* MRS. BAKER *closes the door behind her.*

MRS. BAKER   I'm glad I found you in, Donny.

DON   Jill, this is my mother.

JILL   Your mother? Have I been here a month?

DON   Mother, this is . . . Mrs. Benson.
(MRS. BAKER *studies* JILL *from head to toe with ill-concealed disapproval*)

JILL   How do you do?

MRS. BAKER   (*Coolly*)   How do you do, Mrs. Benson? Are you living here, too?

JILL   I live next door. I just stopped in to ask Don to . . . er . . . I had trouble zipping up my blouse.

MRS. BAKER   So I see. Where *is* your blouse?

JILL   (*Looking around*)   It's here somewhere. (*She sees it on the floor and rushes to get it*) There it is. You see I have this long zipper in the back. It's hard to do alone.
(JILL *scrambles into her blouse.* MRS. BAKER *picks up* DON's *clothes and places them on his lap*)

51

MRS. BAKER Put your things on.

DON (*Rises and dresses*) All right, Mom, what are you doing here? We had an agreement.

MRS. BAKER I was in the neighborhood . . .

DON You were at Saks, which is on 50th Street and Fifth Avenue. This is 11th Street between Second and Third.

MRS. BAKER I bought you some shirts, and I thought you'd have them sooner if I brought them myself.

DON I don't need any shirts. You just brought them as an excuse to come down here.
(JILL *goes to* MRS. BAKER *and turns her back to be zipped*)

JILL Would you mind?
(MRS. BAKER *glares daggers at* JILL's *back, but zips up the blouse as she looks around the room*)

MRS. BAKER And this is what you left home for?

DON This is it.

MRS. BAKER It isn't Buckingham Palace, is it?

DON No, it's the Taj Mahal.
(MRS. BAKER *moves around, stopping to look at the "picnic" things on the floor*)

MRS. BAKER Is this where you eat—on the floor?

DON It's fun eating on the floor, Mom. You ought to try it.

(*A withering glance from* MRS. BAKER *is* DON's *reply.* MRS. BAKER *takes in the sofa and chairs*)

MRS. BAKER Where did this furniture come from?

DON Some of it came with the apartment and some of it I picked up in a junk shop.

MRS. BAKER Don't tell me which is which. Let me guess. (MRS. BAKER *goes to* JILL's *door and looks inside, in disbelief*) What in God's name is this?

DON I don't know what you're looking at.

JILL That's my apartment.

MRS. BAKER Have you ever thought about hiring a maid, Mrs. Benson?

JILL I can manage. I may be sloppy, but I'm not dirty. There's a difference between sloppy and dirty.

MRS. BAKER I'm so glad to hear that.

DON So she's not Craig's wife.

MRS. BAKER Has this door always been open?

DON No, it's always been locked. I opened it this morning.

MRS. BAKER What on earth *is* that?

DON Now what are you looking at?

MRS. BAKER   That's what I'd like to know.

JILL   It's your bed.

DON   My bed.

JILL   Isn't that wonderful?

MRS. BAKER   (*Looking the bed over, incredulously*) You actually sleep up there?

DON   Like a baby.

MRS. BAKER   What happens if you fall out?

DON   I go to the ladder and climb up again.

MRS. BAKER   Where are your clothes?

DON   There's a closet and chest in the bathroom.

MRS. BAKER   And where is the bathroom—under the bed?

DON   That's right.

MRS. BAKER   Of course it is.
(MRS. BAKER *exits to the bathroom.* JILL *rushes to* DON)

JILL   Boy, were you ever right!

DON   About what?

JILL   She never had syphilis. I'm surprised she had you. Why did you introduce me as Mrs. Benson?

DON I don't know. It makes you sound . . . more important.

> (*Offstage we can hear the sound of the toilet flushing*)

JILL What is she doing?

DON Testing the plumbing. She's a nut about plumbing.

JILL Sssh! How did you know it was your mother when she came in? She didn't make a sound.

DON (*Sniffing the air*) Smell. (JILL *sniffs the air*) It's called Numéro Dix and she uses half a bottle at a time. I always know when she's around.

JILL It's like having a bell on a cat. (*Offstage we hear the sound of drawers opening and closing*) Now what is she doing?

DON Checking the drawers to see if I have enough socks and underwear. She's a nut about socks and underwear. What she's really doing is gathering up evidence to hit me with and try to make me come home. I was so sure she'd walk in and say, "I could absolutely cry." She let me down.

JILL She's not finished. She'll say it.

DON No, she'd have said it by now. I know all her routines.

JILL What do you want to bet she says it? How about dinner tonight? If she doesn't say it, we eat in my place and I pay. If she says it, we eat here and you pay.

DON It's a bet, but you might as well start shopping. (MRS. BAKER *enters from the bathroom*)

MRS. BAKER Well, that's some bathroom. No wonder you hide it under the bed.

DON Gee, I thought you were going to say something else.

MRS. BAKER I haven't finished. I haven't even started.

DON Well, say it and get it over with.

MRS. BAKER Well, there's only one thing *to* say.

JILL (*Aside to* DON) Here it comes.

MRS. BAKER Perhaps it's a blessing that you can't see what you're living in.

DON Right, Mom. I count that blessing every time I come in the door.

MRS. BAKER Donny, can I be honest?

DON *Can* you?

JILL (*Aside to* DON) This is it.

MRS. BAKER I am shocked and appalled.

JILL I lose. Seven-thirty all right?

DON   Perfect.

MRS. BAKER   There's no tub in your bathroom.

DON   It's under the dining table.

MRS. BAKER   I could absolutely cry!

DON   (*To* JILL)   You win! Hamburgers all right?

JILL   But at least two each.

MRS. BAKER   I am not just talking about this rat hole, Donny, I am talking about you, too. You're so thin. You've lost weight.

DON   I haven't lost anything. I'm exactly the right weight for my height—six-one—and my age—eleven.

MRS. BAKER   (*Goes to the refrigerator*)   I'd like to see what you're eating. (*She opens it and looks in, carefully*) There's nothing in here but lettuce . . . and an apple.

JILL   Where?

MRS. BAKER   Behind the lettuce.

DON   I knew there was another one.
   (MRS. BAKER *closes the refrigerator and turns back into the room. Her appraising glance falls on* JILL. *She stares at her for a moment;* JILL *grows uncomfortable*)

MRS. BAKER   Tell me, where is *Mr.* Benson?

JILL Who's Mr. Benson?

MRS. BAKER I assumed he was your husband.

JILL Oh, Jack. I don't know. Last time I saw him he was sitting outside of Hamburger Hamlet on the Strip. Why?

MRS. BAKER I was curious about your marital status.

JILL I haven't any.

DON Jill is divorced.

MRS. BAKER How old are you, Mrs. Benson?

JILL Nineteen.

MRS. BAKER Nineteen? And you've already been married and divorced?

JILL Yeah...And now I'm allowed to vote.

MRS. BAKER I think you should be allowed to run. How long were you married?

JILL Six days.

MRS. BAKER And on the seventh day you rested?

JILL No, I split. I have to change now. I have an audition.

MRS. BAKER An audition for what?

DON   A play. An off-Broadway play.

MRS. BAKER   I was speaking to Mrs. Benson.

JILL   A play. An off-Broadway play.

MRS. BAKER   Then, you're an actress.

JILL   Well . . . yes.

MRS. BAKER   Might I have seen you in anything—besides your underwear?

JILL   Not unless you went to Beverly Hills High School. I was in *The Mikado*. I played Yum Yum.

MRS. BAKER   Yes, I'm sure you did.

JILL   And about a year ago I did a TV commercial for Panacin.

MRS. BAKER   What is Panacin?

JILL   You know, it's for acid indigestion.

MRS. BAKER   No, I don't know. One of the few problems I *don't* have is acid indigestion.

DON   There are givers and there are takers.

MRS. BAKER   You're asking for it, Donny. (*To* JILL) Does your mother know where you are?

JILL   Sure.

MRS. BAKER   And does she approve of the way you're living?

JILL   What "way" am I living?

DON   Mom, are you conducting some kind of a survey?

MRS. BAKER   And you're going to get it. I'm sure Mrs. Benson doesn't mind answering a few questions. Do you, Mrs. Benson?

JILL   Well, I have this audition . . .

MRS. BAKER   What does your father do?

JILL   Which one?

MRS. BAKER   How many fathers have you?

JILL   Four. One real and three steps.

MRS. BAKER   Your mother has been married FOUR times?

JILL   So far. We live in Los Angeles.

MRS. BAKER   Then you come from a broken home.

JILL   Several.

MRS. BAKER   Why does your mother marry so often?

JILL   I don't know. I guess she likes it. I mean she likes *getting* married. Obviously, she doesn't like *being* married. I'd better get started. Okay. See you later, Don.

DON Good luck!

JILL Thanks.

DON Don't forget—seven-thirty here.

MRS. BAKER What happens at seven-thirty here?

DON Jill and I are having dinner together.

MRS. BAKER Mrs. Benson . .

DON Just the two of us. Alone!

MRS. BAKER Mrs. Benson, I think you've forgotten something. (As JILL turns, MRS. BAKER picks up the fall, gingerly, and holds it out to her)

DON What is it?

JILL Susan Potter's hair.
    (JILL takes the fall and exits to her apartment, closing the door)

DON Did you have to be so goddamn rude?

MRS. BAKER Was I rude?

DON All those questions! What are you—the Attorney General of Scarsdale?

MRS. BAKER I think I have a right to know something about my son's friends.

DON Let's talk about my rights! You're not supposed to

be here for another month. Why did you have to come today, huh?

MRS. BAKER   Since when do you speak to me this way?

DON   Since when do you come sneaking into my room this way?

MRS. BAKER   I didn't come sneaking in. The door was unlocked.

DON   You could have knocked. I thought it was a raid.

MRS. BAKER   It should have been. Why don't you lock your door?

DON   Until I knew my way around the room, it was easier to let people come in on their own, but it'll be locked from now on.

MRS. BAKER   I thought my coming here would be a pleasant surprise for you. Had I known I'd be treated like the Long Island Railroad—

DON   You'd've come anyway.

MRS. BAKER   And I'm glad I did. My worst fears have been realized.

DON   Thank heaven! *My* worst fear was that *your* worst fears wouldn't be realized. Can you imagine if you came here and liked it? We'd have nothing to talk about.

MRS. BAKER   Did you have to choose such a sordid neighborhood?

62

DON To me it looks just like Scarsdale.

MRS. BAKER There are lots of nice places up in the Sixties and Seventies.

DON I don't trust anybody over 30th Street.

MRS. BAKER I'd be terrified to live with the type of people down here.

DON They've been nice to me.

MRS. BAKER (Glancing at JILL's door) I'll bet they have. This morning you told me you didn't know Mrs. Benson's name.

DON I didn't. I hadn't met her when we talked.

MRS. BAKER You certainly made friends in a hurry, didn't you?

DON She's a very friendly girl.

MRS. BAKER I can see she is. May I ask you a personal question?

DON No.

MRS. BAKER Have you slept with this girl?

DON I thought you'd never ask. Yes, I have.

MRS. BAKER As if I didn't know.

DON If you know, why did you ask?

MRS. BAKER And now I know why you're so anxious to have a place of your own. Not because you want to do something constructive with your life. You just want a place where you can have orgies—night and day!

DON Oh, Mother. Two's company, three's an orgy.

MRS. BAKER I know you, Donny. You've got that Linda Fletcher look on your face again. You're going to fall in love with this girl, too.

DON Maybe I will. Does it bother you that I'm heterosexual?

MRS. BAKER Mrs. Benson is not exactly the sort of girl a mother dreams of for her son.

DON Mom, I'm not interested in the girl of *your* dreams.

MRS. BAKER Obviously a stupid girl.

DON Not at all. She even quotes Dylan Thomas.

MRS. BAKER How wonderful! I can assure you Dylan Thomas never quoted *her*. And she's not at all attractive.

DON Oh, come on now—

MRS. BAKER She has beady little eyes like a bird and a figure like . . . a pogo stick.

DON You've just described the girl of *my* dreams.

MRS. BAKER You can't see the difference between good

and bad. I can see people's faces. I can see into their eyes. You can't.

DON Ah, but I can see past their eyes and into their souls. Leave us not forget Little Donny Dark and all that vision.

MRS. BAKER You don't know what you're talking about. You've never been exposed to life.

DON Whose fault is that? Whose fault is it I didn't go to school with other kids?

MRS. BAKER How could you?

DON There are schools for blind kids.

MRS. BAKER We could afford to have you taught at home. I thought that was better than sending you off with a bunch of blind children like . . . a leper.

DON Is that how you see me—like a leper?

MRS. BAKER Of course not!

DON Come on, Mom, deep, deep down haven't you always been just a little ashamed that you produced a blind child?

MRS. BAKER It's nothing to be ashamed of.

DON Embarrassed, then.

MRS. BAKER You have never given me reason to be embarrassed by you.
(*There is a knock at* JILL's *door*)

65

DON Come in.
(JILL enters in a different outfit. She crosses to
MRS. BAKER *and turns her unzipped back to her)*

JILL I hate to bother you.
(MRS. BAKER zips it up in one contemptuous zip)

DON What's wrong?

JILL Just another zipper. *(She starts toward her door,
stopping to whisper to* DON*)* I think you're winning.
Hang in there! *(To* MRS. BAKER, *sweetly)* Thank you.
(JILL exits to her apartment, closing the door)

MRS. BAKER She'll be a great help to you. She can't
even dress herself.

DON That's where I can help her.
*(MRS. BAKER has been looking at the bed with
interest; she turns to* DON *enthusiastically)*

MRS. BAKER Donny, I have a wonderful idea! You come
on home. I'll have your bed raised—and there's a ladder
in the garage. I'll put up some psychedelic posters . . .

DON Nice try, Mother, but it just wouldn't be the same.

MRS. BAKER All right! If you insist on staying here, I
will not support you.
(DON rushes to the telephone and picks it up)

MRS. BAKER What are you doing?

DON Calling *The Daily News*. What a story! "Florence
Baker refuses to help the handicapped!"

MRS. BAKER (*Grabbing the phone away*) I'm serious, Donny!

DON   Oh, then I'll call *The Times.*

MRS. BAKER   What are you going to do for money? The little you saved must be gone now.

DON   I have some left.

MRS. BAKER   And when that's gone?

DON   I can always walk along the street with a tin cup.

MRS. BAKER   Now, you *are* embarrassing me.

DON   Don't worry, Mom. I'll keep away from Saks.

MRS. BAKER   Just stop all this joking. I want to know what your plans are.

DON   I'm going to sing and play the guitar. I'm pretty good. You've said so yourself.

MRS. BAKER   I didn't know you were planning to make a career of it. Have you any idea of the competition you're facing?

DON   I have just as good a chance as anyone else. Better. I have charisma.

MRS. BAKER   May I ask how you arrived at this brilliant decision?

DON   It was elementary, my dear mother—by the process of elimination. I made a lengthy list of all the things I could *not* do, like, well, like commercial pilot. I don't think TWA would be too thrilled to have me fly their planes, nor United, nor Pan Am. Photographer? A definite out—along with ball player and cab driver. Matador didn't strike me as too promising. I half considered becoming an eye doctor, but that would just be a case of the blind leading the blind. That's a little joke. (*Shrugs when he gets no response*) I said it was little.

MRS. BAKER   I suppose Linda Fletcher put this guitar idea into your head.

DON   You might say she was instrumental. (*Waits for a response to this*) That was another joke, Mom. You'd better start laughing at something or people will think you're a lesbian.

MRS. BAKER   You've certainly picked up some colorful language, haven't you?

DON   You can learn anything down here.

MRS. BAKER (*Goes to the bathroom door*)   Yes. Well, I think you've learned enough, young man. I hardly recognize my own son.
(*She enters the bathroom and brings out a suitcase*)

DON   What are you doing?

MRS. BAKER (*Plunks the suitcase down loudly on a chair*) I'm doing what I should have done long ago. I'm taking you home.

DON   Forget it, Mother. There's no way—

MRS. BAKER You cannot stay here alone!

DON I'm not alone. I have friends.

MRS. BAKER Oh, don't think you've fooled me with all your parties. There are no parties! You have no friends!

DON I have now. I have Mrs. Benson.

MRS. BAKER You'd be better off with a seeing-eye dog.

DON They're not as much fun. Anyway, I've got a seeing-eye mother.

MRS. BAKER (*Snapping open the suitcase*) That's right —and she's taking you home. Mrs. Benson will just have to learn to dress herself.

DON Put that suitcase away!

MRS. BAKER You're coming home, Donny!

DON (*Firmly*) Give me that suitcase! (DON *lunges across to the chair where he heard the suitcase placed.* MRS. BAKER *lifts the suitcase from the chair.* DON *stumbles around trying to find the suitcase*) Where is it? Give me that suitcase, Mother! (*He stands, holding his hand out*) Give it to me! (MRS. BAKER *stands staring at* DON *for a moment, as iron-willed as he. Suddenly, a wave of resignation comes over her. She takes* DON's *hand and places it on the suitcase handle.* DON *grabs the handle, carries the suitcase to the bathroom, opens the door, throws the bag in, and closes the door. His tension ebbs and he goes over to his mother*) Mom, please stop worrying about me. I'm going to be all right. If the music doesn't work out, I can always study law

or technology. There are lots of things blind people can do now. So, don't worry any more. (*He reaches his hand out to find her.* MRS. BAKER *takes his hand and places it on her face.* DON *kisses her cheek*) Well, I have to go, Mom. Thanks for dropping by.
(*He crosses to his jacket and walking stick*)

MRS. BAKER   Where are you going?

DON   I have to do some shopping. I told you, I'm having dinner in tonight . . . with Mrs. Benson . . . just the two of us—*alone.*

MRS. BAKER   I'll wait till you come back.

DON   I don't want you to wait. Have a nice trip back to Scarsdale and I'll call you tomorrow. Now, please. I don't want to smell you here when I get back.

MRS. BAKER   I was planning to stay for dinner.

DON   Your plans have changed. Like I said, it's me and Mrs. Benson, just the two of us—*alone.*

MRS. BAKER   And after dinner, I suppose an orgy.

DON (*Opening the front door*)   I hope so. At last the sinister truth is revealed—Little Donny Dark is just a dirty old man!
(DON *makes a clicking sound, winks and exits.* MRS. BAKER *looks around the room with frustration. She goes over to the picnic lunch, picks up the dishes, puts them on a tray, carries them to the kitchen and sets them down*)

MRS. BAKER (*Mumbling to herself*)   Mrs. Benson!

JILL (*Opening her door*) Yes?
(MRS. BAKER *is startled for a moment, but recovers quickly*)

MRS. BAKER (*In sweet, dulcet tones*) Could you come in for a moment, Mrs. Benson?

JILL (*Uneasily*) Well, I have my audition. I should leave in about fifteen minutes. I don't know New York and I get lost all the time.

MRS. BAKER (*Ingratiatingly*) Don't you worry. I'll see that you get off in time. (JILL *enters, reluctantly*) I thought you and I might have a little talk. You know, just girls together. Please sit down. (JILL *remains standing, avoiding too-close contact with* MRS. BAKER) Would you like a cup of coffee? tea?

JILL No, thank you. But if that apple is still there . . .

MRS. BAKER I'm sure it is.

JILL Where's Don?

MRS. BAKER (*Opening the refrigerator and taking out the apple*) Shopping. (*She washes the apple in the sink, and polishes it with a dishtowel*) You must be so careful to wash fruits and vegetables, you know. They spray all those insecticides on everything now. I'm not at all sure the bugs aren't less harmful. I like apples to be nice and shiny.
(MRS. BAKER *holds the apple out to* JILL, *who looks at it and then at* MRS. BAKER, *oddly*)

JILL This reminds me of something. What is it?

71

MRS. BAKER I have no idea.

JILL You . . . handing me the apple . . . nice and shiny . . . Oh, I know! Snow White. Remember when the witch brought her the poisoned apple? I'm sorry. I didn't mean that the way it sounded. I know you're not a witch.

MRS. BAKER Of course not. And I know you're not Snow White.
(JILL *takes the apple*)

JILL I may have to wait hours before I read. I'll probably starve to death before their eyes.

MRS. BAKER You're going to get that part, you know.

JILL What makes you so sure?

MRS. BAKER Well, you're a very pretty girl and that's what they want in the theater, isn't it?

JILL Today you have to have more than a pretty face. Anyway, I'm not really pretty. I think I'm interesting-looking, and in certain lights I can look sort of . . . lovely, but I'm not pretty.

MRS. BAKER Nonsense! You're extremely pretty.

JILL (*Laughs*) No, I'm not.

MRS. BAKER Yes, you *are*.

JILL No, I'm not. I've got beady little eyes like a bird, and a figure like a pogo stick. (*She waits for a reac-*

tion from MRS. BAKER. *There isn't one*) Well? Aren't you going to deny you said that?

MRS. BAKER (*Unperturbed*) How can I, dear? Obviously, you heard it.

JILL There are plenty of true things you can put me down with. You don't have to put me down with lies.

MRS. BAKER You know what I like about you?

JILL Nothing.

MRS. BAKER Oh, yes. I like your honesty . . . your candor. You're really quite a worldly young woman, aren't you, Mrs. Benson?

JILL I suppose I am. I wish you wouldn't call me Mrs. Benson.

MRS. BAKER That's your name, isn't it? Mrs. Benson?

JILL But you don't say it as though you mean it.

MRS. BAKER I'm sorry. Why don't I call you Jill? That's more friendly—and I'll try to say it as though I mean it. Now, Jill, you were telling me about your childhood.

JILL I was?

MRS. BAKER It must have been interesting having so many fathers.

JILL Well, it was, actually. All mother's husbands were so different, so I was exposed to all kinds of ideas about life, and world affairs—even religion. My real father was a Methodist. My next father was a Christian Scientist. The next was Jewish and the last one was Episcopalian.

MRS. BAKER That covers just about everything. Doesn't your mother like Catholics?

JILL Oh, yes, she likes them, but for some reason Catholics are not allowed to marry her.

MRS. BAKER I would imagine she's got an X-rating from the church.

JILL Too bad. She's really very nice.

MRS. BAKER I'm sure she is. So it's your childhood that has made you so worldly and understanding.

JILL Yes, and being so worldly and understanding, Mrs. Baker, I can tell that you didn't ask me here to discuss my childhood or to tell me how pretty I am.

MRS. BAKER I was interested in seeing what you and Donny might have in common. He likes you very much.

JILL And I like him very much. He may very well be the most beautiful person I've ever met. Just imagine going through life never seeing anything . . . not a painting, or a flower, or even a Christmas card. I'd want to die, but Don wants to live. I mean really *live*. And he can even kid about it. He's fantastic.

MRS. BAKER Then you would want what's best for him, wouldn't you?

JILL   Now we're getting to it, aren't we? Like maybe I should tell him to go home with you. Is that it?

MRS. BAKER   Donny was happy at home until Linda Fletcher filled him with ideas about a place of his own.

JILL   Maybe you just want to believe that he can only be happy with you, Mrs. Baker. Well, "There are none so blind as those who will not see." There. I can quote Dylan Thomas AND Little Donny Dark.

MRS. BAKER   You constantly astonish me.

JILL   Well, we women of the world do that.

MRS. BAKER   Funny how like Linda you are. Donny is certainly consistent with his girls.

JILL   Why do you call him Donny?

MRS. BAKER   It's his name. Don't I say it as though I mean it?

JILL   He hates being called Donny.

MRS. BAKER   He's never mentioned it.

JILL   Of course, he has. You just didn't listen. There are none so deaf as those who will not hear. You could make up a lot of those, couldn't you? There are none so lame as those who will not walk. None so thin as those who will not eat—

MRS. BAKER   Do you think it's a good idea for Donny to live down here alone?

JILL   I think it's a good idea for *Don* to live wherever he wants to . . . and he's not alone. I'm here.

MRS. BAKER   For how long? Have you got a lease on that apartment?

JILL   No.

MRS. BAKER   So, you can leave tomorrow if you felt like it.

JILL   That's right.

MRS. BAKER   You couldn't sustain a marriage for more than six days, could you?

JILL   (*Upset*)   My marriage doesn't concern you.

MRS. BAKER   It didn't concern you much, either, did it?

JILL   Yes, it did!

MRS. BAKER   Have you thought about what marriage to a blind boy might be like? Let's face it, not even your mother has covered THAT territory!

JILL   Suppose we leave my mother out of this, huh?

MRS. BAKER   I'm sorry. I didn't know you were so touchy about her.

JILL   I'm not touchy about her. I just don't want to talk about her.

MRS. BAKER   All right. We'll talk about you. Look, Jill, you've seen Donny at his best—in this room, which he's memorized. And he's memorized how many steps to the drugstore, and to the delicatessen. But take him out of this room or off this street and he's lost; he panics. Donny needs someone who will stay with him —and not just for six days.

JILL You can stop worrying, Mrs. Baker. Nothing serious will develop between Don and me. I'm not built that way!

MRS. BAKER But Donny *is* built that way.

JILL Oh, please—we're just having kicks.

MRS. BAKER Kicks! That's how it started with Linda— just kicks. But Donny fell in love with her . . . and he'll fall in love with you. Then what happens?

JILL I don't know!

MRS. BAKER Then don't let it go that far. Stop it now before you hurt him.

JILL What about you? Aren't you hurting him?

MRS. BAKER I can't. I can only irritate him. You can hurt him. The longer you stay, the harder it will be for him when you leave. Let him come with me and you go have your kicks with someone who won't feel them after you've gone!
      (JILL *turns to face* MRS. BAKER, *studying her intently*)

JILL I'm not so sure you can't hurt him. Maybe more than anybody. I think you deserve all the credit you can get for turning out a pretty marvelous guy. But bringing up a son—even a blind one—isn't a lifetime occupation. Now the more you help him, the more you hurt him. It was Linda Fletcher—not you—who gave him the thing he needed most: confidence in himself. You're always dwelling on the negative—always what he needs, never what he wants; always what he can't do, never what he can. What about his music? Have you heard the song he wrote? I'll bet you didn't even know he could write songs! You're probably dead right about me. I'm not the ideal girl for Don, but I know one thing—neither are you! And if I'm going to tell anyone to go home, it'll be you, Mrs. Baker. YOU go home!

(JILL *turns*)

Curtain

The scene is the same, that night. The dining table is set for two, with JILL's *basket of flowers and some lighted votive candles on it.* DON *is adjusting the silverware on the table.* MRS. BAKER *is in the kitchen, noisily looking through a cabinet.*

DON Oh, Mom, what are you doing in there?

MRS. BAKER I'm looking for some wax paper to wrap the meat in so it doesn't spoil.

DON I haven't any wax paper and the meat won't spoil.

MRS. BAKER This meat looks terrible.

DON Who asked you to look at it. Why don't you get out of the kitchen?

MRS. BAKER What time is it? Midnight?

DON (*Feeling his braille watch*) It's only twenty to ten.

MRS. BAKER *Only* twenty to ten?

DON I know. She's undependable and unreliable. She's uneverything. What else is new?

MRS. BAKER You did say seven-thirty. I heard you.

DON Listen, you don't have to hang around, you know.

79

MRS. BAKER I'll just wait until she comes. (*Going to the tape recorder*) I'm not going to interfere with your orgy. I told you that.

DON No, I told you that. (MRS. BAKER *turns the tape recorder on.* DON's *singing and playing of "Butterflies Are Free" is heard.* MRS. BAKER *listens, impressed. Moving toward* JILL's *door*) Mom, please turn it off. I want to hear if she comes in.

MRS. BAKER Is that the song you wrote?

DON Yes . . . well, it's not finished. (*Thinks for a second*) How'd you know I wrote it?

MRS. BAKER I didn't. I just asked you.

DON Oh.

MRS. BAKER It's good. Pretty.

DON You mean pretty good?

MRS. BAKER No, I mean good and pretty.

DON Wow.
(DON *turns toward his mother with some surprise as he moves away from* JILL's *door*)

MRS. BAKER Where do you suppose she is?

DON Probably still auditioning.

MRS. BAKER For six hours? I'm worried about her.

DON (*Even more surprised*) *You're* worried about *Jill?*

MRS. BAKER Aren't you?

DON Something's come over you. First you like my song, now you're worried about Jill. (*He thinks for a moment, then turns to her*) And you haven't mentioned my coming home for hours. Are you all right?

MRS. BAKER Don't I seem all right?

DON No. You're not behaving like Supermom. Next thing you'll be telling me you like Jill.

MRS. BAKER I don't dislike her. I just wish she were a different sort of girl.

DON She *is* a different sort of girl. That's what you don't like.

MRS. BAKER When I was her age, punctuality meant something.

DON What did it mean?

MRS. BAKER It meant that if I were going to be three hours late for dinner, I'd call and explain.

DON You would never be three hours late.

MRS. BAKER No, I certainly would not!

DON You'd be a month early.

MRS. BAKER You know, she might be lost. She said she always loses her way around New York.

DON Any cab driver could bring her home. (*With a*

quizzical look) She never said she loses her way around New York.

MRS. BAKER   Oh, yes—she said it to me.

DON   If she'd said it to you, I'd've heard it.

MRS. BAKER (*Flustered*) Well . . . I guess it was after you went out.

DON   She was in here while I was out?

MRS. BAKER   It seems to me she was . . . yes.

DON   Why?

MRS. BAKER   Oh, the usual—she wanted her dress zipped up.

DON   You did that while I was here.

MRS. BAKER   She just stopped in, that's all. She was only here a minute.

DON   What did you talk about?

MRS. BAKER   I don't remember.

DON   You remember she loses her way around New York. What else did you talk about?

MRS. BAKER   What does it matter?

DON (*Raising his voice*) If it doesn't matter, then tell me!

82

MRS. BAKER Donny, please don't shout at me! (*After a moment*) We talked about Snow White.

DON Snow White and the Seven Dwarfs? *That* Snow White?

MRS. BAKER Is there any other?

DON Why were you talking about her?

MRS. BAKER (*Irritated*) What difference does it make why we were talking about Snow White? We didn't say anything bad about her.

DON I don't like you talking to my friends behind my back.

MRS. BAKER It wasn't behind your back! You weren't even in the room! (*She is thoughtful for a moment as she slips off her earrings*) Donny? Did Linda Fletcher give you confidence?

DON Mother, you know damn well what Linda Fletcher gave me, so don't be funny.

MRS. BAKER I wasn't being funny. Did she *also* give you confidence?

DON Yes.

MRS. BAKER Didn't *I*?

DON You gave me help.

MRS. BAKER I always thought one led to the other.

DON Not necessarily, I guess.

MRS. BAKER Why didn't you tell me you don't like being called Donny?

DON I told you a thousand times.

MRS. BAKER I'd remember something I heard a thousand times.

DON Maybe it was only a hundred. What's this all about? Why all these questions?

MRS. BAKER What's wrong with "Donny"?

DON It reminds me of Little Donny Dark.

MRS. BAKER And what's wrong with that?

DON You work on it.

MRS. BAKER Well, what would you like to be called? I'll try to remember.

DON Don . . . Donald. You can call me Sebastian or Irving. I don't care. Anything but Donny.

MRS. BAKER I'm not going to call you Sebastian or Irving. I'll try to remember to call you—
      (*She is interrupted by a faint noise from* JILL's *apartment. They both turn toward* JILL's *door. The noise grows louder; it is laughter and conversation, none of it intelligible. We hear* JILL's *voice and a man's*)

84

DON (*Smiling*) She's home! She'll be in in a minute. You can go now, Mom.
(MRS. BAKER *goes near* JILL's *door and listens*)

MRS. BAKER There's a man with her.

DON Stop listening at the door.

MRS. BAKER I can't hear anything. They're at the other end, but there's a man with her.

DON That's probably the television you hear.

MRS. BAKER Why should she be laughing and talking with a television set?

DON Mom, please come away from there.
(MRS. BAKER *moves away from* JILL's *door, noticing that* DON *is anxious*)

MRS. BAKER I am away from there.
(*There is a loud, whimsical knock at* JILL's *door*)

DON Come on in!
(JILL *enters, gaily, followed by* RALPH AUSTIN, *a young man, sloppily dressed*)

JILL Oh, hi! I'm back! I've brought Ralph Austin with me. (*Seeing* MRS. BAKER) Oh, Mrs. Baker—you're still here. (*Making introductions*) Don, this is Ralph Austin. I told you about him. He's directing the play. Ralph, this is Don, and Don's mother, Mrs. Baker. (*They exchange how-do-you-do's*) I told Ralph all about you and he was anxious to meet you.

RALPH (*In an unnaturally loud voice*) Hey, Jill told

85

me how with-it, how . . . how adept you are for someone who's . . . well, for someone who can't see.

DON You can say "blind," Ralph. It's in my vocabulary,
too.

RALPH Oh, yes. (*Shouting*) I should have known that.
Jill told me you have no hang-ups about the thing.

DON Ralph, you don't have to shout.

MRS. BAKER Mr. Austin, my son is not deaf!

RALPH (*In a normal tone*) Oh. I'm sorry.

DON It happens all the time. People think if you can't
see, you can't hear.

JILL He can hear a lot better than we can.

DON No, I can't.

JILL And what sense of smell!
(*She looks at* MRS. BAKER)

MRS. BAKER Can I fix you something before I go?

RALPH We've had dinner, but I wouldn't mind some
coffee if it isn't too much trouble.

MRS. BAKER You were expected here for dinner, Jill.
(JILL *looks over at the dining table and crosses
to it, unhappily*)

JILL Oh, Don . . . I'm sorry.

DON It's all right.

JILL Our flowers and candles. It's so beautiful. (*She turns back, concealing her upset with flippancy*) Well, there you are. That's me for you. I just completely forgot. We went to Ralph's place after the audition to celebrate and we drank a whole bottle of champagne or whatever it was.

RALPH It was sparkling burgundy.

DON (*Excitedly*) Then you got the part?

JILL Yes and no. I'm not playing the wife.

DON What are you playing, the homosexual?

JILL No, his secretary. It's a small part, but I've got one good scene.

RALPH Jill did a really great audition. Man, I was really proud of her.

JILL God, was I nervous. It wasn't the reading, but imagine having to stand out there completely and totally naked.
(MRS. BAKER *drops a cup, which breaks*)

MRS. BAKER Sorry, I broke a cup.

JILL Can I help you?

MRS. BAKER (*Picking up the pieces*) No, thank you. It's already broken. How many coffees?

DON None for me.

JILL I don't want any.

DON Why did Jill have to be naked for the audition?

RALPH Because there's a lot of nudity involved in this play. We had to see the actors' bodies. The *visual* here is very important. I hope you don't mind my saying that.

DON Not at all.

MRS. BAKER How do you take your coffee, Mr. Austin?

RALPH Just black, please.

JILL Now I don't think anyone can call me a prude.

MRS. BAKER I'd like to see them try.

JILL At first I hated the idea of getting completely undressed, but there were like forty or fifty actors all around me, all naked. I was the only one with clothes on. (*Turning to* MRS. BAKER) How would you feel?

MRS. BAKER (*Handing* RALPH *his coffee*) Warm—all over!

RALPH I was out front with the writer and the producer, and the minute we saw Jill naked we knew she wasn't right for the lead.

MRS. BAKER Tell me, Mr. Austin, is there any story to this play or is that too much to hope for?

RALPH It has a very dramatic story, Mrs. Baker.

JILL   I die at the end.

MRS. BAKER   Pneumonia?

RALPH   It's going to be a wild scene. I'm a genius at this kind of thing. Jill will be lying there on the stage dying of an overdose of heroin. She's in agony, writhing across the stage on her back—screaming this one word. She screams it over and over and over and over.

DON   What's the word?

MRS. BAKER   Did you have to ask?

RALPH   Well, uh . . . I don't know if I should use it here.

MRS. BAKER   You're going to use it on the stage, but you don't know if you should use it *here?*

DON   That's all right, you can say it. What's the word? (RALPH *crosses and whispers into* DON's *ear.* DON *squirms slightly)* Maybe you'd better not.
   (MRS. BAKER *sighs with relief)*

DON   Ralph, do you think the public is ready for this kind of thing.

RALPH   Are you kidding? They're dying for it. I'm talking about the *thinking* public—not those giddy little tight-assed matrons from Scarsdale. (*Everyone freezes.* RALPH *slowly becomes aware of the chill in the room)* Have I said something wrong?

MRS. BAKER   Pick anything, Mr. Austin.

JILL Ralph, Mrs. Baker lives in Scarsdale.

RALPH Oh. (*Trying, with a big smile*) Well, present company excepted, isn't that the rule?

MRS. BAKER I don't wish to be excepted, thank you. Tell me, what's the name of your play?

RALPH It's called *Do Unto Others*.

MRS. BAKER I must remember that; I'd hate to wander in by accident.

JILL You might like it if you gave it a chance, Mrs. Baker. I mean see it with an open mind.

DON I should warn you my mother hasn't liked anything since *The Sound of Music*.

JILL The play isn't really dirty. I wouldn't be in a dirty play. It's true to life.

DON Not Mom's life.

JILL This play is really good. It just needs polishing.

MRS. BAKER I'd've said scrubbing.

RALPH (*He sits next to* JILL, *intimately*) We'll just have to try to make it without the support of Scarsdale.

MRS. BAKER Well, I wouldn't count on this giddy little matron. I don't intend to pay money to see nudity, obscenity and degeneracy.

RALPH Mrs. Baker, these things are all a part of life.

MRS. BAKER I know, Mr. Austin. So is diarrhea, but I wouldn't classify it as entertainment.

JILL Listen, Ralph, if this play is going to be closed by the police . . .

RALPH Don't worry. It'll run two years and I wouldn't be surprised if it made a star out of you.

JILL Wouldn't it be groovy to see JILL TANNER up in lights?

MRS. BAKER Jill Tanner?

JILL Benson is my married name, but I'm using my real name—Tanner. Please remember it. I mean it would be terrible if I became a star and nobody knew it was me.

RALPH (*Rising*) I've got to get going. Steve is coming over with some rewrites. How long will it take you to pack?

JILL (*With an anxious glance at* DON) Well . . . not long, but you go ahead.

RALPH I'll wait if you're not going to take forever. How many bags have you got?
     (*A troubled look comes to* DON's *face.* MRS. BAKER *looks at* DON, *concerned for him*)

JILL Only two, but it'll take me a while to find things.

RALPH I can only let you have one closet.

DON Are you going somewhere?

JILL Didn't I tell you? I'm moving in with Ralph. I thought I mentioned it.

MRS. BAKER No, you didn't.

JILL Well, Ralph thought it would be a good idea to move in with him.

RALPH It was your idea.

JILL It doesn't matter whose idea it was. It was a good one. (*To* DON) I'm not really moving away, Don. I mean it's not far from here. (*To* RALPH) Where is it?

RALPH Off Christopher Street.

JILL Is that far?

RALPH Across town.

JILL See? Ralph has a terrific studio apartment. Something like this, with a skylight. He hasn't got a bed like yours, but it's really great. Wait till you see it. I mean, we want you to come over whenever you like. Don't we, Ralph?

RALPH Sure. We'll consider you one of the family.

JILL (*To* RALPH) I told you you'd like Don. (*To* DON) We'll have some groovy times over there. You're going to love Ralph. He's one of *us*. I wish you could see him. He has a good face. I mean strong and noble. Let Don feel your face. He can tell what you look like by feeling your face. It's really a kind face.

RALPH   Go ahead, Don.

MRS. BAKER   He doesn't want to, Mr. Austin.
(JILL *takes* DON's *hand and places it on* RALPH's
face. DON *runs his fingers over* RALPH's *face. He
pulls his hand away, quickly*)

RALPH   Well, it's been great meeting you, Don. See you
soon, I hope. Don't take long, hon. Oh, nice to have
met you, Mrs. Baker. I apologize if I offended you.

MRS. BAKER   That's quite all right, Mr. Austin. I assure
you it won't happen again.

RALPH (*To* JILL, *with a parting gesture*)   Hon.
(RALPH *exits through the front door, leaving* JILL,
DON *and* MRS. BAKER *all looking away from each
other in embarrassed silence*)

JILL   Well, I'd better start packing. I'll stop in and say
good-bye before I leave.
(JILL *exits to her apartment, hurriedly, closing
the door behind her.* MRS. BAKER *looks at* DON,
almost unable to bear the hurt on his face)

DON   Mom? (MRS. BAKER *doesn't answer; she stares at*
DON, *thoughtfully*) Mom, are you here?

MRS. BAKER   Yes.

DON   I have something to tell you. You'd better sit down.

MRS. BAKER   Is it something awful?

DON   No, you'll like it, but you'd better sit down.

MRS. BAKER *(Remains standing)* I'm sitting.

DON I want to go home. Will you get the car, and I'll pack. Did you hear me?

MRS. BAKER Yes.

DON Why don't you say something?

MRS. BAKER I intend to. I'm collecting my thoughts.

DON Can't you do that while you get the car? I won't take long.
(He starts toward the bathroom)

MRS. BAKER Just a minute. (DON *turns back*) I think we ought to talk about it.

DON *Talk* about it? I thought you'd be dancing with joy about it. Isn't that what you wanted? Isn't that why you came here today—to take me home?

MRS. BAKER Yes.

DON Then what is there to talk about? God, we've been talking about it all day. You said this place isn't Buckingham Palace. You said I was living in a rat hole.

MRS. BAKER And you said it's the Taj Mahal. You said this is your home now. Why aren't *you* dancing with joy?

DON Are you saying you don't want me to come home?

MRS. BAKER No. I'm only saying we should talk about it. Don't misunderstand me. I still think this place is

94

dreadful and I doubt if I'll ever like it, but I didn't choose to live here. You did. You couldn't wait to have a place of your own. You rushed into this and now you want to rush out. I think we should talk about it.

DON   Isn't it funny that we think exactly alike, but never at the same time. I . . . I can't make it now, Mom. I'm not going to make it.

MRS. BAKER   Why? Because a girl has walked out on you?

DON   Two girls. Let's don't forget Linda.

MRS. BAKER   And it may be ten girls. Girls walk out on sighted men, too, you know.

DON   Is that supposed to make me feel better?

MRS. BAKER   It's supposed to make you stop feeling sorry for yourself. You've never felt sorry for yourself before. Please don't start now. You're going to meet a lot of girls. One day you'll meet one who is capable of a permanent relationship. Jill isn't. She knows this herself. I think you're better off staying here. I don't want you coming home discouraged and defeated. You've got your music.

DON   Christ, once and for all get it into your head—I am not Little Donny Dark! I *am* discouraged! I *am* defeated! It's over!

MRS. BAKER   Do you remember the first Donny Dark story?

DON   No.

MRS. BAKER   You were five years old. We were spending
the summer on Lake Winnipesaukee. Dad took you
into the lake. It was the first time you'd been in any
water deeper than a bathtub. You were terrified. They
could hear you screaming all over New Hampshire.
Dad brought you in and I put you to bed. You trembled
for hours. That night I told you a story about a little
blind boy who could swim the seven seas and could
talk to the dolphins—

DON   (*Remembering, bitterly*) Yeah, and the dolphins
told him about enemy submarines on their way to de-
stroy the United States Navy, and Donny Dark swam
home in time to save them. What a lot of crap.

MRS. BAKER   The next day you learned to swim! I didn't
write those stories hoping for a Pulitzer Prize in litera-
ture. I wrote them because I found a way to help you.
Whenever you felt discouraged or defeated, I told you
a Donny Dark story, and then you tried a little harder
and you did a little better. Shall I make one up now—
or are you man enough to handle this situation yourself?

DON   A month ago *you* didn't think I was man enough.
You said I wasn't ready to leave home. Why have you
changed?

MRS. BAKER   I don't know that *I've* changed. *You're*
not the boy who left home a month ago. I came down
here today hoping you *were*. It's hard to adjust to
not being needed any more. But I can do it now. So
you get on with your own life. (*Looking around the
room for a moment*) I'd like to see you have some decent
furniture. You need some dishes and some glasses. I
don't use all those at home. I'll send some down to you.

DON Okay.

MRS. BAKER And I'll send some linens. You could use better ashtrays. If you fix this place up, it might not be so bad. (*Hesitantly*) Can I help you fix it up a little?

DON Sure.

MRS. BAKER I'll call you in the morning and we'll talk about it.

DON Mom. I'm glad you came.

MRS. BAKER (*Looks at him for a moment, then kisses him, gently, on the cheek*) I love you, Don.

DON I know, Mom. I know you do. (MRS. BAKER *leaves.* DON *crosses to* JILL'S *door and listens for a moment. He pulls himself out of his despair and raps at the door, gaily*) Hey! How you doin'?
(JILL *opens the door and enters carrying two suitcases*)

JILL (*Setting the bags down*) I think I made it. Listen, I left those new dishtowels there, and the light bulbs, if you want them.

DON I don't need them.

JILL Well, I'll donate them to the apartment. Oh, and here's the key. (*She takes a key from her pocket, crosses to the coffee table and puts it down*) I'll leave it here on the table. Will you give it to the super? I guess you'd better have him lock this door again.

DON   I'll wait and see who moves in. It might be someone groovy.

JILL   Oh. Yeah. I hope so. Well, let's don't have a big good-bye or anything. I'll be in touch with you.

DON   Can't you stay a minute?

JILL   Well . . . once I'm going somewhere, I like to get going. You know what I mean?

DON   I'm the same way. I was just going to have a corned beef sandwich on rye. Want one?

JILL   Once I'm going somewhere, I like to get going— unless someone offers me a corned beef sandwich on rye.

DON   How 'bout a beer?

JILL   Sure. (*She crosses to the dining table*) The candles are still lit.

DON   (*As he is fixing the beer and sandwich*)   I know. I'm very religious.

JILL   Where's Mama?

DON   She went home.

JILL   I didn't hear her leave. What was the verdict? (*JILL sits on the table, resting her feet on a chair. She takes a cigarette from her bag and lights it*)

DON   She accepted my declaration of independence.

JILL You're kidding!

DON I must say she put up a great battle.

JILL Maybe she should've won. I mean . . . maybe you would be better off at home.

DON That's a switch!

JILL I've been thinking about it.

DON Come on, girl. It took me a whole day and three pints of blood to convince my mother. I don't want to start on you.

JILL I like to have things done for me.

DON Then give up Ralph and the play and move in with my mother. I'm out of mustard.
(DON *comes out of the kitchen, slightly disoriented, and almost collides with a stool*)

JILL I don't care. What do you think of Ralph?

DON (*Looking up, surprised*) Where are you?

JILL I'm on the sofa.

DON Oh. I couldn't figure where your voice was coming from.

JILL You always could before.

DON I . . . I wasn't concentrating. (*Handing her the plate*) He seemed very nice.

JILL Who?

DON Ralph.

JILL You didn't like him, did you?

DON I said he seemed very nice.

JILL I could tell you didn't like him. You were a little uptight when he was here.

DON I'm always a little uptight when there's more than one person in the room. I have to figure out who's speaking and if he's speaking to me.

JILL I guess you didn't like him because he was rude.

DON (*Sitting on an arm of the sofa*) Was he rude?

JILL Well, you know, putting down Scarsdale like that to your mother.

DON That was an accident. He didn't know she was from Scarsdale. I'm sorry you think he's rude.

JILL I don't think he's rude.

DON Well, you said it. I didn't. (*Looking around*) Or is there someone else here?

JILL I know he comes off as a little conceited.

DON Tell me, Jill, do *you* like Ralph?

JILL (*With a self-conscious laugh*) What kind of a question is that? I'm moving in with him, aren't I? Why would I move in with a guy I didn't like?

DON   That was my next question.

JILL   I'd better be going . . .

DON   (*Rising quickly*)   Come to think of it, I guess I don't like Ralph.

JILL   I knew it all along. But why?

DON   Like you said—he's rude and conceited.

JILL   But I've been trying to tell you he's not like that. I knew that's what you thought, but he's not at all conceited.

DON   And thanks a lot for making me feel his face.

JILL   I thought you might like him better if you knew what he looked like. He's got a good face.

DON   To look at, maybe, but it doesn't come across to the touch.

JILL   I'm sorry about that. I hoped we could all be friends. Well, I'd better—

DON   (*Quickly*)   You know something? I'm going to tell you something. *You* don't like Ralph.

JILL   Oh, God! I just packed two suitcases which are sitting right over there so I can move in with him!

DON I don't care if you have thirteen trunks! You don't like him.

JILL Boy, you really are too much! You think just because you're blind you can see everything!

DON That's right—that sixth sense we've got tells me you don't like Ralph Austin! How about that? Spooky, isn't it?

JILL No, it's just stupid. I packed two suitcases which are sitting right over there—

DON Tell me, with Ralph is it like the Fourth of July and like Christmas?

JILL Not exactly, but he has a kind of strength. With him it's more like . . . Labor Day.

DON Do you think *he's* a beautiful person, too?

JILL In many ways, yes.

DON Has he got charisma?

JILL Definitely!

DON Then I'm selling mine.

JILL You'd better hurry. It's been known to fade away.

DON Do you love him?

JILL Why should I answer that? No matter what I say, you've already made up your own mind about it.

DON Go ahead, answer it! Do you love him?

JILL Yes! In my way.

DON This morning you told me you could never love anyone.

JILL That was this morning. Am I allowed to change my mind or has my first statement already been passed into law by Congress?

DON Look, I'm not the worldliest human being on the block, but I know that when you're rushing into the arms of the man you love, you don't stop for a corned beef sandwich on rye.

JILL Which shows how little you know me. Some people wear their hearts on their sleeves—I wear my appetite.

DON Was it something my mother said?

JILL Was *what* something your mother said?

DON The reason you're leaving. The reason you didn't show up for dinner. I know you didn't forget. Was it something my mother said?

JILL *You* don't even listen to your mother. Why should I?

DON Then why are you leaving? And don't give me that crap about loving Ralph.

JILL I'm leaving because I want to leave. I'm free and I go when I want to go.

DON   I thought it might have something to do with me.

JILL   It has nothing whatsoever to do with you.

DON   Okay. (JILL *lights a cigarette, plops down on the sofa and looks at* DON, *disturbed*) You're scared to death of becoming involved, aren't you?

JILL   I don't want to get involved. I told you that.

DON   That's right, you told me. No responsibility, no commitments.

JILL   I have to be able to get out if I get tired of the—

DON   Tired of me?

JILL   Or anybody.

DON   What if I got tired of you?

JILL   (*This hadn't occurred to her*) Of me?

DON   Doesn't anyone ever get tired of you?

JILL   I don't hang around long enough to find out.

DON   With Ralph, you could get out any time you feel like it, but it might be harder to walk out on a blind guy, right?

JILL   The blindness has nothing to do with it. Nothing!

DON   You know goddamn well it has! You wouldn't feel a thing walking out on Ralph or Sebastian or Irving, but if you walked out on Little Donny Dark, you might hate yourself and you wouldn't like that, would you? Hate *me*—or love *me*—but don't leave because I'm blind, and don't stay because I'm blind!

JILL Who are Sebastian and Irving?

DON Nobody. I just made them up.

JILL Sometimes I don't understand you. We don't think alike and I know I'd only hurt you sooner or later. I don't want to hurt you.

DON Why not? You do it to others. Why do I rate special treatment?

JILL I don't want to be another Linda Fletcher. She hurt you, didn't she?

DON She helped me, too. She was there when I needed her.

JILL I can't promise that. I don't know where I'll be when you need me.

DON You need me a helluva lot more than I need you!

JILL I don't need anybody. I never did and I never will. I have to go now.

DON I'm glad you said *have* to and not *want* to.

JILL Boy, I finally said something right. I'll be seeing you.

DON Yeah, I'll be seeing you. I'll think about you for

years and wonder if you ever made a commitment, if you ever got involved.

JILL I hope not.

DON Don't worry. It won't happen—because you're emotionally retarded. Did you know that? That's why you couldn't face marriage. It's why you can't face anything permanent, anything real. You're leaving now because you're afraid you might fall in love with me, and you're too adolescent for that responsibility. And you're going to stay that way. Oh, God, I feel sorry for you—because you're crippled. I'd rather be blind.

(JILL *leaves, closing the door behind her.* DON *stands motionless for a few seconds, then dazedly takes a few steps backward. He brushes against the arm of the sofa, which jolts him a bit. Orienting himself, he turns, goes to the dining table, and starts to clear it. Some silverware clatters to the floor; he makes a move to pick it up, but doesn't bother to complete the gesture. Instead he carries some dishes to the kitchen sink. Suddenly an idea strikes him and he makes his way across the room to the tape recorder, and fumblingly turns it on. His voice is heard singing: "And you made me understand/ Right from the start/ I could hold your gentle hand/ But never hold your heart/ So why the crying?/ Were our brave words lying/ When we both agreed there'd be no tears in our good-byeing?" As if to escape the painful memory, he begins to wander around the room. When he comes up against the table he feels for the heat of the candles and bends down to blow them out; as he does so his face accidentally brushes against the flowers, and he buries his face in them for a moment. But then he rips the flowers out of the basket, and with one sweep knocks everything on the table to the floor. The gesture causes him to bump into a stool, which he hurls across the room. Staggering aimlessly, he stumbles over the sofa, and falls headlong onto the floor. One arm is pinned under him. He lies there with tears welling in his eyes, and no interest in getting up. Finally he gropes for the coffee table to raise himself, but gives up and sinks back down, weeping. The front door opens.* JILL *enters, carrying her bags. She looks around the room for* DON. *When she sees what has happened, she suppresses a scream, and sets down her bags abruptly.* DON *hears this; startled and aware of his helpless position he whirls around on the floor. Anxiously)* Who is it? . . . Who's there?

JILL *(There is a silence, then she breaks the tension)* The news is good. It's not your mother.

DON *(Realizing it's* JILL, *and attempting to compose himself)* What are you doing here?
(She crosses to him, sits beside him on the floor, and takes his hand)

JILL *(Kissing his hand)* What are you doing on the floor?

DON Oh . . . I was about to have a picnic.

JILL *(Brightly)* What a great idea—
(He turns to her, and she begins to laugh. Hesitant at first, DON *joins in the laughter. He reaches out for her and they hug each other joyfully)*

Curtain

107

About the Author

LEONARD GERSHE has worked in the theater in London and New York, and on TV scripts and motion pictures in Hollywood. He wrote the original screenplay *Funny Face,* which won him an Academy Award nomination. With Leonard Spigelgass he wrote the screen version of the Cole Porter musical *Silk Stockings.* Both films were on *The New York Times'* ten best pictures list for 1957. In 1959 Mr. Gershe authored the book for the Broadway musical *Destry Rides Again.* Several years of writing songs and screenplays followed; then he returned to the theater, his first love.

One morning Mr. Gershe was listening to a radio interview with a blind Harvard law student who was chuckling over the fact that his draft board had classified him 1-A. "I had never met a blind person, and was bowled over by this boy's humor and healthy attitude about his situation," the author says. Mr. Gershe had also been thinking about the personality of a friend of his, a young Hollywood star who was wary of committing herself to any permanent relationship. He was intrigued by the idea of bringing these two characters together in a play. And so *Butterflies Are Free* came to be.